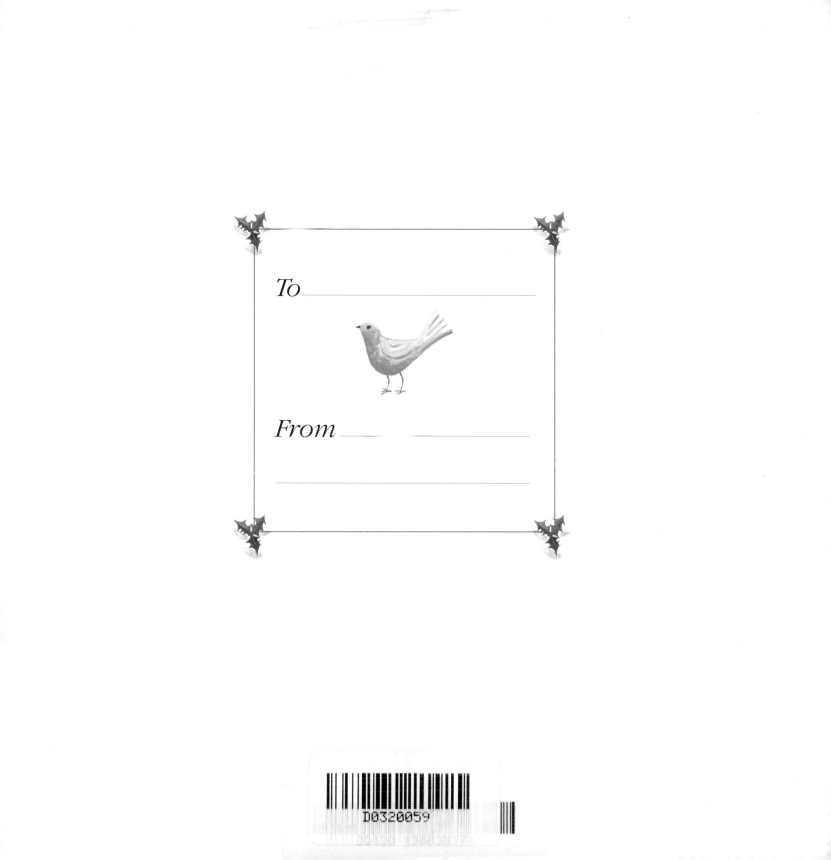

To _____

From _____

_____

To James, with love P.T. and V.T.
To Emily, Charlotte and Holly D.L.

The Lion Book of
Christmas Carols

Arrangements by Philip and Victoria Tebbs
Illustrated by Debbie Lush

LION
CHILDREN'S

Carol arrangements copyright © 1998 Philip and Victoria Tebbs
Illustrations copyright © 1998 Debbie Lush
Story text copyright © 1998 Lion Hudson
This edition copyright © 2004 Lion Hudson
Designed by Nicky Jex

The authors assert the moral right
to be identified as the authors of this work

A Lion Children's Book
an imprint of
Lion Hudson plc
Mayfield House, 256 Banbury Road,
Oxford OX2 7DH, England
ISBN 0 7459 4918 5

First published in hardback edition in 1998 as *Best-Loved Carols*
First edition 2004
1 3 5 7 9 10 8 6 4 2 0

Acknowledgments
Story text adapted from the Bible.
Music of 'O Little Town of Bethlehem' ('Forest Green')
collected and adapted by Ralph Vaughan Williams.
Simplified arrangement used by permission of
Oxford University Press.

A catalogue record for this book is available
from the British Library

Printed and bound in Singapore

Contents

Introduction

*C*hristmas is a very special time of year—a time for being together to celebrate the wonder of Jesus' birth, a time of feasting and of gifts… it is a season of gold amidst the grey of winter.

Long ago and far away, people were dreaming that one day an age of gold would dawn.

For sometimes it seemed that their lives were more bleak and dreary than any winter. Enemies had defeated their nation, and their overlords seemed cruel and unfair.

If only they could return to the times of the great King David of old, who had led their people to victory and prosperity… If only the God who had made heaven and earth would remember them, and send them a king even greater than David, who would rule with justice and righteousness, who would put an end to war, whose kingdom would never end.

Then the whole world would see that God wanted people to live freely and fairly, with kindness, compassion, justice and generosity.

The whole world would know an age of gold.

Deck the Hall

Words and Tune: Traditional Welsh

Deck the hall with boughs of hol-ly, *Fa la la la la, la la la la,*

D   G   D/A   A   D

'Tis the sea-son to be jol-ly, *Fa la la la la, la la la la,*

G   D/A   A   D

Don we now our gay ap-pa-rel, *Fa la la, la la la, la la la,*

A   D   A   D   Bm   A/E   E7   A

Troll the an-cient yule-tide car-ol, *Fa la la la la, la la la la.*

D   G   D/A   A   D

Deck the hall with boughs of holly,
Fa la la la la, la la la la,
'Tis the season to be jolly,
Fa la la la la, la la la la,
Don we now our gay apparel,
Fa la la, la la la, la la lu,
Troll the ancient yuletide carol,
Fa la la la la, la la la la.

See the blazing yule before us,
Fa la la la la, la la la la,
Strike the harp and join the chorus,
Fa la lu la la, la la la la,
Follow me in merry measure,
Fa la la, la la la, la la la,
While I tell of yuletide treasure,
Fa la la la la, la la la la.

Fast away the old year passes,
Fa la la la la, la la la la,
Hail the new, ye lads and lasses,
Fa la la la la, la la la la,
Sing we joyous all together,
Fa la la, la la la, la la la,
Heedless of the wind and weather,
Fa la la la la, la la la la.

Jingle Bells

Words and Tune: James Pierpont

Jin - gle Bells! Jin - gle Bells! Jin - gle all the way! Oh, what fun it

G C

is to ride In a one-horse op - en sleigh! Oh! Jin - gle Bells! Jin - gle Bells!

C G A7 D G

Jin - gle all the way! Oh, what fun it. is to ride In a one-horse op - en

C G D

Fine

sleigh! Dash - ing through the snow In a one-horse op - en sleigh

G C

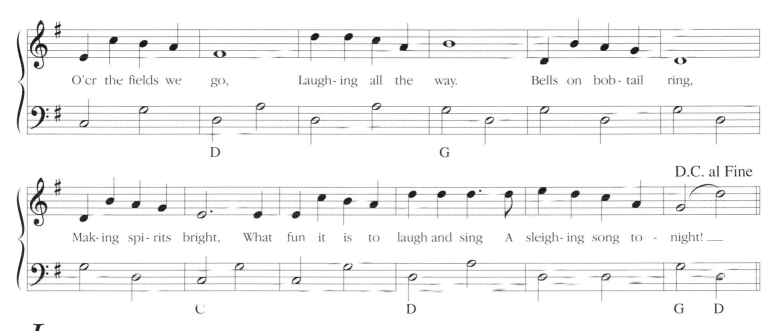

O'er the fields we go, Laugh-ing all the way. Bells on bob-tail ring,

D   G

D.C. al Fine

Mak-ing spi-rits bright, What fun it is to laugh and sing A sleigh-ing song to - night! —

C   D   G   D

Jingle Bells! Jingle Bells!
Jingle all the way!
Oh, what fun it is to ride
In a one-horse open sleigh! Oh!
Jingle Bells! Jingle Bells!
Jingle all the way!
Oh, what fun it is to ride
In a one-horse open sleigh!

Dashing through the snow
In a one-horse open sleigh
O'er the fields we go,
Laughing all the way.
Bells on bob-tail ring,
Making spirits bright,
What fun it is to laugh and sing
A sleighing song tonight!

Jingle Bells! Jingle Bells!
Jingle all the way!
Oh, what fun it is to ride
In a one-horse open sleigh! Oh!
Jingle Bells! Jingle Bells!
Jingle all the way!
Oh, what fun it is to ride
In a one-horse open sleigh!

A Message from an Angel

❧

The angel Gabriel was sent by God to a town in Galilee called Nazareth, to a young woman named Mary. She was not yet married, but she was engaged to a man named Joseph. His family could trace their ancestors back a thousand years, to a great king of their nation: King David.

'Peace be with you,' said the angel to Mary. 'The Lord is with you and has greatly blessed you.'

Mary was much perplexed. What did these words mean?

'Do not be afraid, Mary,' said the angel. 'God has chosen you to bear a son. You will name him Jesus. He will be great; he will be called the Son of the Most High, and God will make him a king like his ancestor David. His kingdom will never end.'

'How can this be?' asked Mary. 'I am a virgin—not yet married.'

'The power of God will make all this happen,' replied the angel. 'For this reason, the child to be born will be holy; he will be called the Son of God.'

Then Mary said, 'I am the Lord's servant. May it happen to me as you have said.'

The angel departed.

Luke 1:26–38

Gabriel's Message

Words: Sabine Baring-Gould (1834–1924)
Tune: Traditional Basque

The an - gel Ga - bri - el from hea - ven came, ___ His wings as
Am · · · · · · · G · Esus4 · E · Am

drift - ed snow, his eyes ___ as flame; ___ 'All hail,' said he, 'thou
D · Esus4 · Am · · C

low - ly mai - den Ma - - - ry, ___ Most high - ly fav - oured
Am · · Dm · F · G · · Dm

la - dy.' Glo - - - - - - - ri - a! ___
Esus4 · E · F · C · D · Esus4 · Am

The angel Gabriel from heaven came,
His wings as drifted snow, his eyes as flame;
'All hail,' said he, 'thou lowly maiden Mary,
Most highly favoured lady.' Gloria!

'For known a blessèd mother thou shalt be,
All generations laud and honour thee,
Thy son shall be Emmanuel, by seers foretold,
Most highly favoured lady.' Gloria!

Then gentle Mary meekly bowed her head,
'To me be as it pleaseth God,' she said.
'My soul shall laud and magnify his holy name.'
Most highly favoured lady, gloria!

Of her, Emmanuel, the Christ, was born
In Bethlehem, all on a Christmas morn,
And Christian folk throughout the world will ever say,
'Most highly favoured lady, gloria!'

The Baby Born in Bethlehem

Mary told Joseph her news about the angel's visit and the baby she was now expecting. Joseph was dismayed and perplexed. What should he do? The baby was not his; perhaps he ought not to marry Mary.

Then, in a dream, he too was visited by an angel. 'Joseph,' said the angel, 'do not be afraid to take Mary as your wife. The child she will bear is God's holy child. You must name him Jesus, for he will rescue people and show them the right way to live.'

Matthew 1:18–21

So Joseph took care of Mary. When the Roman emperor Augustus ordered a census of all the people who lived in his empire, Joseph took Mary with him to enter their names on the official list.

Everyone had to travel to their home town. As Joseph was descended from the nation's great King David, who had been born in Bethlehem, it was there that they made their way.

When they arrived, they found the town was crowded with people who had come to take part in the census. The inn was full. Mary and Joseph had to shelter in a stable, among the animals. There, Mary's baby son was born. She wrapped him in swaddling bands and laid him in a manger.

Luke 2:1–7

O Little Town of Bethlehem

Words: Bishop Phillips Brooks (1835–93)
Tune: Collected and adapted by Ralph Vaughan Williams (1872–1958)

O lit - tle town of Beth - le - hem, How still we — see thee

G   D   G   D   G   C   D

lie! A - bove thy deep and dream - less — sleep The si - lent — stars go

G   D   G   D   G   C   D

by. Yet — in thy dark — streets — shin - eth The ev - er - last - ing

G   Bm   C   D   Em   D   G   C

light; The hopes and fears of all — the — years Are met in — thee to - night.

D   G   D   G   D   G   C   D   G

O little town of Bethlehem,
How still we see thee lie!
Above thy deep and dreamless sleep
The silent stars go by.
Yet in thy dark streets shineth
The everlasting light;
The hopes and fears of all the years
Are met in thee tonight.

O morning stars, together
Proclaim the holy birth,
And praises sing to God the King,
And peace to men on earth;
For Christ is born of Mary;
And gathered all above,
While mortals sleep, the angels keep
Their watch of wondering love.

How silently, how silently,
The wondrous gift is given!
So God imparts to human hearts
The blessings of his heaven.
No ear may hear his coming;
But in this world of sin,
Where meek souls will receive him, still
The dear Christ enters in.

O holy child of Bethlehem,
Descend to us, we pray;
Cast out our sin, and enter in,
Be born in us today.
We hear the Christmas angels
The great glad tidings tell:
O come to us, abide with us,
Our Lord Emmanuel.

Mary Had a Baby

Words and Tune: Traditional West Indian

Ma - ry had a ba - by, Yes, Lord. _ Ma - ry had a ba - by, Yes, my Lord.

F   C7   F   C7

Ma - ry had a ba - by, Yes, Lord. The peo - ple keep a - com - ing And the train done gone.

F   B♭   Am   F   G7   C7   F

Mary had a baby,
Yes, Lord.
Mary had a baby,
Yes, my Lord.
Mary had a baby,
Yes, Lord.
The people keep a-coming
And the train done gone.*

What did she name him?
Yes, Lord.
What did she name him?
Yes, my Lord.
What did she name him?
Yes, Lord.
The people keep a-coming
And the train done gone.

Mary named him Jesus,
Yes, Lord.
Mary named him Jesus,
Yes, my Lord.
Mary named him Jesus,
Yes, Lord.
The people keep a-coming
And the train done gone.

Where was he born?
Yes, Lord.
Where was he born?
Yes, my Lord.
Where was he born?
Yes, Lord.
The people keep a-coming
And the train done gone.

Born in a stable,
Yes, Lord.
Born in a stable,
Yes, my Lord.
Born in a stable,
Yes, Lord.
The people keep a-coming
And the train done gone.

Where did Mary lay him?
Yes, Lord.
Where did Mary lay him?
Yes, my Lord.
Where did Mary lay him?
Yes, Lord.
The people keep a-coming
And the train done gone.

Laid him in a manger,
Yes, Lord.
Laid him in a manger,
Yes, my Lord.
Laid him in a manger,
Yes, Lord.
The people keep a-coming
And the train done gone.

* Some people sing 'Down in Bethlehem' to replace 'And the train done gone'.

Silent Night

Words: Joseph Mohr (1792–1848)
Translation from German: Anonymous
Tune: Franz Grüber (1787–1863)

Si - lent night, ho - ly night, All is calm,

C   G7

All is bright Round yon vir - gin moth - er and child;

C   F   Dm   C

Ho - ly in - fant so ten - der and mild, Sleep in hea - ven - ly

F   Dm   C   G   G7

peace, _____ Sleep ___ in hea - ve - nly peace.

C   G7   C

Silent night, holy night,
All is calm, all is bright
Round yon virgin mother and child;
Holy infant so tender and mild,
Sleep in heavenly peace,
Sleep in heavenly peace.

Silent night, holy night,
Shepherds quake at the sight;
Glories stream from heaven afar,
Heavenly hosts sing alleluia;
Christ, the Saviour, is born,
Christ, the Saviour, is born.

Silent night, holy night,
Son of God, love's pure light
Radiant beams from thy holy face,
With the dawn of redeeming grace,
Jesus, Lord, at thy birth,
Jesus, Lord, at thy birth.

Away in a Manger

Words: Anonymous
Tune: W.J. Kirkpatrick (1838–1921)

A - way in a ___ man - ger, no ___ crib for a bed, The ___

F   Dm   Gm

lit - tle Lord Je - sus laid ___ down his sweet head. The

C7   F   Dm   Gm   G7   C

stars in the ___ bright sky looked ___ down where he lay, The ___

F   Am   Dm   Gm

lit - tle Lord Je - sus a - sleep on the hay.

C   F   Gm   C   F

Away in a manger, no crib for a bed,
The little Lord Jesus laid down his sweet head.
The stars in the bright sky looked down where he lay,
The little Lord Jesus asleep on the hay.

The cattle are lowing, the baby awakes,
But little Lord Jesus, no crying he makes.
I love thee, Lord Jesus! Look down from the sky,
And stay by my side until morning is nigh.

Be near me, Lord Jesus, I ask thee to stay
Close by me for ever, and love me, I pray.
Bless all the dear children in thy tender care,
And fit us for heaven to live with thee there.

The Shepherds on the Hillside

*O*n the hillsides that sloped down from Bethlehem, some shepherds were spending the night outside, watching over their flocks. Suddenly, one of God's angels appeared before them, shining with all the glory of heaven.

The men cowered in fear but then the angel spoke to them: 'Do not be afraid. I come with good news: news of something that will bring joy to everyone in the world. This very day in David's town has been born a saviour, the one promised by God to lead people to freedom… the one who is to be called the Christ.

'Here is a sign for you, so you will know that what I say is true. You will find the baby wrapped in swaddling clothes and lying in a manger.'

Suddenly a great number of heaven's angels appeared, singing a song of praise: 'Glory to God in highest heaven, peace on earth and goodwill to all people.'

When the angels went back to heaven, the shepherds looked at one another with astonishment. 'Let us go to Bethlehem,' they said, 'and see for ourselves.'

So they went, and found Joseph and Mary and the baby lying in the manger. The shepherds told their strange story, and all who heard it were amazed. Mary thought long and deeply about every word they had said.

The shepherds went back to their flocks, singing praises to God.

Luke 2:8–20

The First Nowell

Words and Tune: Traditional English

The first Nowell, the angel did say, Was to certain poor shepherds in fields as they lay; In fields where they lay keeping their sheep, On a cold winter's night that was so deep. Now-ell, Nowell, Nowell, Nowell, Nowell, Born is the King of Israel!

The first Nowell, the angel did say,
Was to certain poor shepherds in fields as
they lay;
In fields where they lay keeping their
sheep,
On a cold winter's night that was so deep.

Nowell, Nowell, Nowell, Nowell,
Born is the King of Israel!

They looked up and saw a star,
Shining in the east, beyond them far;
And to the earth it gave great light,
And so it continued both day and night.

Nowell, Nowell, Nowell, Nowell,
Born is the King of Israel!

And by the light of that same star,
Three wise men came from country far;
To seek for a king was their intent,
And to follow the star wherever it went.

Nowell, Nowell, Nowell, Nowell,
Born is the King of Israel!

This star drew nigh to the north-west;
O'er Bethlehem it took its rest,
And there it did both stop and stay
Right over the place where Jesus lay.

Nowell, Nowell, Nowell, Nowell,
Born is the King of Israel!

Then entered in those wise men three,
Full reverently upon their knee,
And offered there in his presence
Their gold and myrrh and frankincense.

Nowell, Nowell, Nowell, Nowell,
Born is the King of Israel!

Then let us all with one accord
Sing praises to our heavenly Lord,
That hath made heaven and earth of
naught,
And with his blood mankind hath bought.

Nowell, Nowell, Nowell, Nowell,
Born is the King of Israel!

While Shepherds Watched Their Flocks

Words: Nahum Tate (1652–1715)
Tune: Este's Psalter (1592)

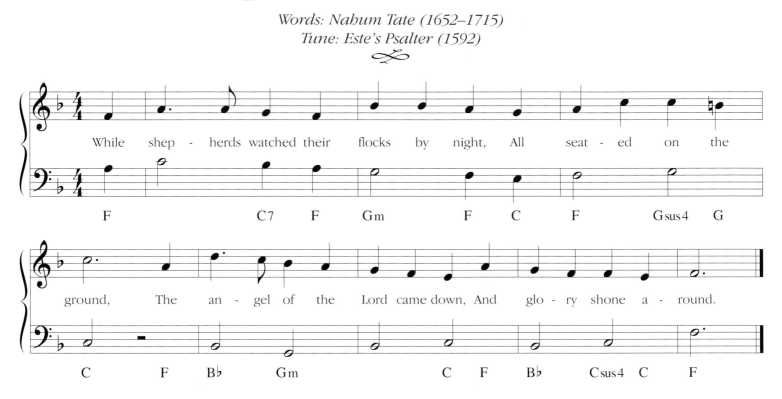

While shep - herds watched their flocks by night, All seat - ed on the

F · · · C7 · F · Gm · F · C · F · Gsus4 · G

ground, The an - gel of the Lord came down, And glo - ry shone a - round.

C · F · B♭ · Gm · · C · F · B♭ · Csus4 · C · F

While shepherds watched their flocks by night,
All seated on the ground,
The angel of the Lord came down,
And glory shone around.

'Fear not,' said he, for mighty dread
Had seized their troubled mind;
'Glad tidings of great joy I bring
To you and all mankind.

'To you in David's town this day
Is born of David's line
A saviour, who is Christ the Lord;
And this shall be the sign:

'The heavenly babe you there shall find
To human view displayed,
All meanly wrapped in swathing bands,
And in a manger laid.'

Thus spake the seraph, and forthwith
Appeared a shining throng
Of angels praising God, who thus
Addressed their joyful song:

'All glory be to God on high,
And on the earth be peace;
Goodwill henceforth from heaven to men
Begin and never cease.'

Hark! The Herald Angels Sing

Words: Charles Wesley (1707–88)
Tune: Felix Mendelssohn (1809–47)

Hark! the herald angels sing
Glory to the new-born King,
Peace on earth and mercy mild,
God and sinners reconciled.
Joyful, all ye nations rise,
Join the triumph of the skies,
With the angelic host proclaim,
Christ is born in Bethlehem.

Hark! the herald angels sing
Glory to the new-born King.

Christ, by highest heaven adored,
Christ the everlasting Lord,
Late in time behold him come,
Offspring of a Virgin's womb.
Veiled in flesh the Godhead see,
Hail the incarnate deity!
Pleased as man with man to dwell,
Jesus, our Emmanuel.

Hark! the herald angels sing
Glory to the new-born King.

Hail, the heaven-born Prince of Peace!
Hail the Sun of Righteousness!
Light and life to all he brings,
Risen with healing in his wings.
Mild he lays his glory by,
Born that man no more may die,
Born to raise the sons of earth,
Born to give them second birth.

Hark! the herald angels sing
Glory to the new-born King.

The Travellers from Distant Lands

Jesus was born in Bethlehem at the time when a man named Herod ruled as king of the Jewish people. Soon afterwards, some men who studied the stars came from lands in the east to the capital city of Jerusalem, where Herod had his palace.

The travellers were on a quest. 'Where is the baby born to be the king of the Jews?' they asked. 'We saw his star rise in the eastern skies, and we have come to worship him.'

When Herod heard this, he was disturbed and angry. He called together the learned people of his nation and spoke to them: 'Our ancient scriptures speak of a king whom God will send. Where will this king be born?'

'In Bethlehem,' they replied. 'A prophet of long ago names the very place.'

Then Herod called the travellers to a secret meeting. He wanted to know when the star had appeared. In return, he told the men to go to Bethlehem. 'Go and search for the child,' he said, 'and when you have found him, let me know, so that I too can go and worship him.'

The travellers went on their way. The star reappeared in the sky, and led them further on, until it stopped over a house in Bethlehem. There they found the child with his mother Mary. They gave the child rich gifts: gold and frankincense and myrrh.

Afterwards, God spoke to them in a dream. 'Go back to your country by a different road,' came the warning. 'Do not go back to Herod.'

Matthew 2:1–12

We Three Kings

Words and Tune: John Henry Hopkins (1820–91)

We three kings of O - ri - ent are; Bear - ing gifts we tra - vel a - far.

Em · B7 · Em · B7 · Em

Field and foun - tain, moor and moun - tain, fol - low - ing yon - der star. O _____

D · G · Am · Em/B · B · Em · D7

star of won - der, star of night, Star with roy - al beau - ty bright,

G · C · G · C · G

West - ward lead - ing, still pro - ceed - ing, Guide us to thy per - fect light.

Em · D · C · D · Em · G · C · G

We three kings of Orient are;
Bearing gifts we travel afar
Field and fountain, moor and mountain,
Following yonder star.

O star of wonder, star of night,
Star with royal beauty bright,
Westward leading, still proceeding,
Guide us to thy perfect light.

Melchior:
Born a king on Bethlehem plain,
Gold I bring to crown him again,
King for ever, ceasing never
Over us all to reign.

O star of wonder, star of night,
Star with royal beauty bright,
Westward leading, still proceeding,
Guide us to thy perfect light.

Caspar:
Frankincense to offer have I,
Incense owns a deity nigh;
Prayer and praising, all men raising,
Worship him, God most high!

O star of wonder, star of night,
Star with royal beauty bright,
Westward leading, still proceeding,
Guide us to thy perfect light.

Balthazar:
Myrrh is mine, its bitter perfume
Breathes a life of gathering gloom;
Sorrowing, sighing, bleeding, dying,
Sealed in the stone-cold tomb.

O star of wonder, star of night,
Star with royal beauty bright,
Westward leading, still proceeding,
Guide us to thy perfect light.

Glorious now behold him arise,
King and God and sacrifice,
Alleluia, alleluia,
Earth to the heavens replies.

O star of wonder, star of night,
Star with royal beauty bright,
Westward leading, still proceeding,
Guide us to thy perfect light.

Good News for All the World

The time came for Joseph and Mary to take Jesus to the Temple in Jerusalem, to give thanks to God for their child.

In Jerusalem there lived an old man named Simeon. He was a good man, and he longed for the day when God would bring his people a saviour. He was quite sure that God would not let him die until he had seen God's chosen one.

At God's prompting, Simeon went to the Temple on the same day that Mary and Joseph came with the baby Jesus. Simeon took the child in his arms and gave thanks to God.

'Lord, you have kept your promise, and now I, your servant, can die in peace. With my own eyes I have seen your saviour, the one who will lead the whole world into your glorious light and bring glory to our people.'

Luke 2:22–32

Joy to the World!

Words: Isaac Watts (1674–1748)
Tune: G.F. Handel (1685–1759)

Joy to the world! the Lord is come;
Let earth receive her King.
Let every heart prepare him room,
And heaven and nature sing,
And heaven and nature sing,
And heaven, and heaven and nature sing.

Joy to the world! the Saviour reigns;
Let men their songs employ,
While fields and floods, rocks, hills and plains
Repeat the sounding joy,
Repeat the sounding joy,
Repeat, repeat the sounding joy.

He rules the world with truth and grace,
And makes the nations prove
The glories of his righteousness
And wonders of his love,
And wonders of his love,
And wonders, wonders of his love.

O Come, All Ye Faithful

Translation from Latin: F. Oakley (1802–80)
Tune: John Francis Wade (1711–86)

O come, all ye faith-ful, Joy-ful and tri-um-phant, O come ye, O come — ye to Beth - le - hem; Come and be-hold him, born the King of an - gels. O come, let us a - dore him, O come, let us a - dore him, O come, let us a - dore him, — Christ — the Lord.

O come, all ye faithful,
Joyful and triumphant,
O come ye, O come ye to Bethlehem;
Come and behold him, born the King of
angels.

O come, let us adore him,
O come, let us adore him,
O come, let us adore him, Christ the Lord.

God of God,
Light of light,
Lo! he abhors not the Virgin's womb;
Very God, begotten, not created.

O come, let us adore him,
O come, let us adore him,
O come, let us adore him, Christ the Lord.

Sing, choirs of angels,
Sing in exultation,
Sing, all ye citizens of heaven above:
'Glory to God in the highest.'

O come, let us adore him,
O come, let us adore him,
O come, let us adore him, Christ the Lord.

Yea, Lord, we greet thee,
Born this happy morning,
Jesu to thee be glory given;
Word of the Father, now in flesh appearing.

O come, let us adore him,
O come, let us adore him,
O come, let us adore him, Christ the Lord.

Go Tell It on the Mountain

Words and Tune: Traditional English

Go tell it on the mountain,
Over the hills and everywhere,
Go tell it on the mountain
That Jesus Christ is born.

While shepherds kept their watching
Over wandering flocks by night,
Behold from out of heaven
There shone a holy light.

Go tell it on the mountain,
Over the hills and everywhere,
Go tell it on the mountain
That Jesus Christ is born.

And lo, when they had seen it,
They all bowed down and prayed,
They travelled on together
To where the babe was laid.

Go tell it on the mountain,
Over the hills and everywhere,
Go tell it on the mountain
That Jesus Christ is born.

We Wish You a Merry Christmas

Words and Tune: Traditional English

We wish you a merry Christmas,
We wish you a merry Christmas,
We wish you a merry Christmas
And a happy New Year.

*Good tidings we bring
To you and your kin;
We wish you a merry Christmas
And a happy New Year.*

Now bring us some figgy pudding,
Now bring us some figgy pudding,
Now bring us some figgy pudding,
And bring some out here.

*Good tidings we bring
To you and your kin;
We wish you a merry Christmas
And a happy New Year.*

For we all like figgy pudding,
We all like figgy pudding,
We all like figgy pudding,
So bring some out here.

*Good tidings we bring
To you and your kin;
We wish you a merry Christmas
And a happy New Year.*

And we won't go till we've got some,
We won't go till we've got some,
We won't go till we've got some,
So bring some out here.

*Good tidings we bring
To you and your kin;
We wish you a merry Christmas
And a happy New Year.*